Camp Wild

Written by
Heather Pindar

Illustrated by
Ramona Bruno

Chapter 1

"Uncle Bob, can't this van go any faster?" asked Joe. "It's getting dark already and I'm hungry."

Joe and his sister, Alana, were going on a camping trip with their Uncle Bob, Auntie Sylvia and cousin, Lizzie. They had been trying to find the campsite for hours.

7122

TCN

- 5 SEP 2023

Books should be returned or renewed by the last
date above. Renew by phone **03000 41 31 31** or
online *www.kent.gov.uk/libs*

'Camp Wild'
An original concept by Heather Pindar
© Heather Pindar 2022

Illustrated by Ramona Bruno

Published by MAVERICK ARTS PUBLISHING LTD
Studio 11, City Business Centre, 6 Brighton Road,
Horsham, West Sussex, RH13 5BB
© Maverick Arts Publishing Limited May 2022
+44 (0)1403 256941

A CIP catalogue record for this book is available at the British Library.

ISBN 978-1-84886-881-6

www.maverickbooks.co.uk

This book is rated as: Lime Band (Guided Reading)

"Van?!" said Bob Bumble loudly. "This isn't just a *van*. *This* is the new Supercamper V–1000 Motor Home. She needs to be driven carefully. And if your Auntie Sylvia could read a map properly, we'd be at the campsite by now."

"And if your Uncle Bob could listen properly, we wouldn't be lost," said Sylvia Bumble.

"The satnav on my phone says 'turn round'," said Alana, before taking a photo of Lizzie with her new camera. Lizzie was sleeping in her toddler seat.

"I don't trust satnavs. Annoying bossy things," said Bob. "A bit like someone we know!" Bob added with a wink and a nod towards Sylvia.

Alana and Joe giggled. They were used to Sylvia and Bob arguing.

Sylvia snorted. "Alana's right," she said. "She's very sensible... Look! There's a driveway we can back into."

Bob stopped and backed slowly into the driveway.

Sylvia turned to Joe and Alana with a grin.

"I've seen faster snails!" said Sylvia.

There was a loud thud. Bob groaned. He turned off the engine and pulled up the handbrake.

"Oops! Sorry, Bob," said Sylvia. "I didn't mean to put you off."

Bob grabbed a torch.

"If my Supercamper's new Ultra Bright Blue paint is scratched, I'll..."

He raced around to the back of the Supercamper.

"No scratches, as far as I can see," he shouted at last. "And I think we've found the campsite."

Chapter 2

Everyone looked at the sign on the tall gate.

It said:

CAMP
WILD
OPEN

"Camp Wild. What a great name!" said Joe.

"Not *too* wild, I hope," said Bob. "I don't want any creepy crawlies or foxes getting near the Supercamper V-1000 Motor Home... or me!"

"Dear, oh dear, Bob!" joked Sylvia. "I agree with Joe, Camp Wild sounds great!"

"Alright, alright, Camp Wild it is," said Bob grumpily.

One half of the gate had already been bashed open by the Supercamper's giant back bumper. Sylvia opened the other half of the gate. Bob carefully turned the Supercamper around again and drove in.

"Remember the Countryside Code!" shouted Joe. "Shut all gates."

Sylvia pushed the two halves of the tall gate together and clicked the latch in place.

It was bad luck for the Bumble family that they only saw one half of the sign on the gate. As the gate closed, both halves of the sign came together. The sign said:

CAMP TOWN WILDLIFE PARK
OPEN 10 'til 6

Chapter 3

Bob followed the track through another gate and parked. It was now dark, so Sylvia put up a string of lights.

"We've got the place to ourselves," said Sylvia happily. "We can be as noisy as we like."

The food cooked outdoors tasted delicious. Sylvia played her guitar, and everyone danced.

Alana took more photos and Bob made everyone

laugh with his truly awful singing.

"You sound like an angry donkey," said Sylvia. "Lizzie sings much better!" Lizzie clapped and everyone laughed.

"Shh, listen!" said Joe suddenly. "What's that?" Then everybody heard it—a screech, from somewhere in the darkness.

A dark shape flew out of the bushes and settled on the bonnet of the Supercamper.

"It's a parrot," said Joe. "How strange! It must have escaped from a zoo."

"Shoo! Get off my Supercamper V-1000 Motor Home!" said Bob. Joe clapped his hands, and the parrot flew away.

"Shimzee!"

said Lizzie, pointing into the darkness.

"Shimzee, shimzee, shimzee!"

"No, Lizzie," said Sylvia. "Parrot."

"Shimzee!" said Lizzie more loudly.

"Parrot!" said Sylvia. She sighed. "Time for

bed everyone."

Chapter 4

The beds in the Supercamper were cosy. Everyone

quickly fell asleep.

Later, Joe woke up with a jolt. The Supercamper

was shaking gently. Then it rocked from side

to side for a moment.

He looked outside but he couldn't see anything in the darkness.

"Did you feel that shaking too?" whispered Alana. "I can't sleep. I heard a sort of... snorting and grunting noise."

"It's weird, like something big is out there. Let's tell Sylvia and Bob," said Joe.

Sylvia and Bob were hard to wake.

"What's up?" mumbled Sylvia. "Snorting and grunting? That'll be your Uncle Bob—his snoring has got really bad lately."

"Rocking and shaking?" said Bob. "That'll be your Auntie Sylvia. She's always blundering about in the night to get snacks from the fridge. Go back to bed."

Chapter 5

The next morning, Sylvia, Joe and Alana woke early. They decided to go exploring. It was a chance for Alana to take more photos for the competition she had entered at school.

They followed a path through a grassy field and crossed a bridge over a small stream. They turned a corner and stopped and stared, amazed.

With its spiky mane, chunky body and dazzling stripes, there was no mistaking it. They were looking at a zebra. The zebra lifted its head from the grass and stared back.

"A zebra!" said Sylvia. "What... How...?"

Joe and Alana looked at each other. "It must have escaped from a zoo!" they said together.

Alana took out her camera. She crept towards the zebra and took a photo. "If we get closer, maybe we can get a selfie with the zebra!"

"I've got mints," said Joe.

Joe rustled the paper packet. He held out a mint and stood very still.

Slowly, the zebra took a step towards Joe. Then another, and then one more. It sniffed Joe's hand. With a quick flick of its rubbery lips, the zebra took the mint from Joe's hand.

"Got an amazing pic!" whispered Alana.

Joe, Alana and Sylvia took a few more steps along the path. They looked behind them. The zebra was following them.

"Wow! We're, like, *zebra whisperers*," said Joe.

They carried on walking. Then they heard a slow drumming noise behind them. They turned to look. The path was full of zebras.

The three zebra whisperers began to walk faster. So did the zebras.

"They all want mints!" wailed Alana.

Chapter 6

Joe, Alana and Sylvia started to jog. The zebras

started to trot.

The path turned again. Below them a large lake sparkled in the sun.

Now they were running fast and gasping for breath. The zebras' hooves beat like thunder behind them.

They saw a long wooden jetty that stretched into the water.

"To the jetty!" yelled Sylvia. "We're going to have to swim for it!"

Alana frantically zipped her camera back into its waterproof case. They sprinted along the wooden planks and leapt into the water.

Their feet slammed into the muddy lake bottom. They stood up. The water came up to just above their knees. On the banks of the lake, the zebras began quietly eating grass.

Sylvia, Alana and Joe waded through long grasses and reeds at the edge of the lake. Ahead of them, they could hear some noisy splashing. Then they heard a trumpeting noise they had only ever heard on the TV.

"Sounds like... elephants!" said Joe. "It can't be... can it?"

They waded faster towards the noise.

"It *is* elephants!" said Alana, reaching for her camera case.

The elephants sprayed water over their backs with their trunks. One of them had a bright blue patch across its bottom. It was the same bright blue as the Supercamper V-1000 Motor Home.

Alana looked at Joe.

"They must have escaped from a zoo!" they said together.

"Hmmm," said Sylvia.

When they reached the track, they saw a sign. It had an arrow pointing to the right.

"Let's go left," said Sylvia quickly. "*This* way

please, Joe and Alana. Don't even *think* about

following that arrow."

Jo and Alana looked closer at the sign. There

was some writing below on the arrow pointing

right: **To the lions**.

Chapter 7

When Alana, Sylvia and Joe returned to the Supercamper they saw Lizzie playing on the grass nearby. Uncle Bob was staring furiously at the back of the Supercamper. It looked like a big patch of the bright blue paint had been rubbed off. Alana thought back to the elephant with the blue paint on its bottom. So that's what the rocking in the night was!

Bob scratched his head and looked up.

"You all look like you've had a mud bath!" he said. "What happened?"

"We need to leave right away," said Sylvia.

"Alright, Sylvia," agreed Bob. "I've made breakfast. It's keeping warm in the oven. How about we have a bite to eat first, and you can tell me what's happened."

"Alright, Bob. Thank you," said Sylvia. "We are a bit hungry."

Sylvia opened the door to the Supercamper and shrieked. "Bob! Bob! Come and look at this!"

The Supercamper was full of furry creatures.

They were squatting on the table, lounging on the beds and dangling from the curtain rails.

"Chimpanzees!" yelled Bob.

"OUT! Out this minute! How dare you mess up my Supercamper V-1000 Motor Home!"

Bob clapped his hands and stomped around, shooing the chimpanzees out of the Supercamper.

"Bob's so angry he's forgotten he's afraid of wildlife," said Sylvia.

"Shimzees! Shimzees!" yelled Lizzie.

"Shimzees... chimpanzees!" said Alana. "Lizzie knew all along there were chimps in the bushes."

"Everyone inside. Quick! Eat up your breakfast. Then we're leaving," said Bob. He put toast, muffins and a big pot of beans on the table. "I don't know what's going on here, but it's not safe for us or the Supercamper V-1000 Motor Home. First there was that rubbed-off paint and now those pesky chimps have stolen all my cushions."

"Open the roof window, Joe," said Sylvia. "These muddy clothes stink."

Joe did as he was asked, and everyone hurried over to the table to eat.

"Now tell me," said Bob, "what happened on your walk?"

A shadow fell over the table. Everyone looked up. A giraffe was pushing its head through the open window. Everyone shrank back. In a flash, the giraffe flicked out its very long, black tongue and scooped up some beans from Alana's plate.

"Ewww!" said Alana. "I don't want breakfast anymore. Can we just go?"

"We can't. Look outside, there's lots more of them!" said Sylvia.

Having swallowed the beans, the giraffe swooped down again and licked Bob's neck. Bob shrieked, pushed his chair back and fell on the floor.

"Giraffes are herd animals like the zebras," said Joe. "If we can make the leader go away, the rest will follow. What we need is some sort of horrible noise the giraffe won't like."

"Bob's singing!" said Sylvia. "That should do it.

Come on Bob. Sing like an angry donkey! Or do you want to get licked again?"

Bob sang 'Old MacDonald had a Farm'. It was loud, croaky and *truly awful.*

The giraffe looked worried and pulled its head out of the window.

"It's working!" said Joe, looking outside. "The giraffes are leaving."

Chapter 8

Bob drove quickly along the track to the main gates. Joe opened the gates and clanged them closed again behind the speeding Supercamper. A large, green truck nearly drove into them. Bob screeched to a halt. 'Park Ranger' was written on the truck. The truck driver stopped too and jumped out.

"Are you alright?" she asked.

"Fine, thanks," said Bob. "Are you? Sorry, I was driving too fast."

"Shimzee!" said Lizzie, pointing.

Joe looked towards the back of the Supercamper. Two dark brown eyes stared back at him. It was a chimp! Bob hadn't shooed them all away after all. Joe quickly scooped up the chimp. He placed her gently in the ranger's arms.

"We're sorry," he said.

The ranger's mouth dropped open. She watched in amazement as the Supercamper sped away.

In the Supercamper, no one spoke.

At last, Alana said, "Did you see that sign on the gate? We've been camping in a **WILDLIFE PARK.**"

Everyone nodded. They had seen it.

"Oops!" said Joe, and they all burst out laughing.

Chapter 9

The school hall was packed with people. They had come to see the photos in the competition.

Alana was the clear winner.

Every scary, muddy, licky moment of their wild camping trip was in her pictures. The one with Bob being licked by the giraffe was blown up to double size.

"It's so embarrassing!" said Sylvia. "But I'm glad you won, Alana. What will you do with the prize money?"

"I'm sending it to the wildlife park. To say sorry."

"I've made them a card," said Joe.

"That's nice," said Sylvia. "Bob's nearly finished fixing up the Supercamper. He's bought new cushions as well. We wondered if you two would like to come on another trip. We're thinking diving with sharks or maybe tornado chasing."

"Erm..." said Joe.

"Um..." said Alana.

"Only joking!" said Sylvia. "We're going to the seaside."

"I used to worry about the seagulls," said Bob. "But not anymore."

"So... How about it?" said Sylvia.

"Yes please!" said Alana and Joe together.

Discussion Points

1. Where are the Bumbles trying to go in the beginning?

2. What colour is Bob's Supercamper?
a) Shocking Ruby Red
b) Ultra Bright Blue
c) Super Great Green

3. What was your favourite part of the story?

4. Why were the zebras chasing the Bumbles?

5. Why do you think the giraffe didn't like Bob's singing?

6. Who was your favourite character and why?

7. There were moments in the story when the Bumbles didn't **notice their surroundings**. Where do you think the story shows this most?

8. What do you think happens after the end of the story?

Book Bands for Guided Reading

The Institute of Education book banding system is a scale of colours that reflects the various levels of reading difficulty. The bands are assigned by taking into account the content, the language style, the layout and phonics. Word, phrase and sentence level work is also taken into consideration.

The Maverick Readers Scheme is a bright, attractive range of books covering the pink to grey bands. All of these books have been book banded for guided reading to the industry standard and edited by a leading educational consultant.

To view the whole Maverick Readers scheme, visit our website at

www.maverickearlyreaders.com

Or scan the QR code to view our scheme instantly!

Maverick Chapter Readers
(From Lime to Grey Band)